WITHDRAWN

MILAN PUBLIC LIBRARY
MILAN, OHIO

THE MAN WHO WAS LEFT FOR DEAD

THE MAN WHO WAS LEFT FOR DEAD

Jenny Tripp

Illustrated by Charles Shaw

RAINTREE PUBLISHERS
Milwaukee • Toronto • Melbourne • London

Copyright © 1980, Raintree Publishers Inc.

All rights reserved. No part of this book may be reproduced or utilized in any form or by any means, electronic or mechanical, including photocopying, recording, or by any information storage and retrieval system, without permission in writing from the Publisher. Inquiries should be addressed to Raintree Publishers Inc., 205 West Highland Avenue, Milwaukee, Wisconsin 53203.

Library of Congress Number: 79-21519

1 2 3 4 5 6 7 8 9 0 84 83 82 81 80

Printed and bound in the United States of America.

Library of Congress Cataloging in Publication Data

Tripp, Jenny.
   The Man who was left for dead.

   SUMMARY: The true story of a man's survival after being attacked by a grizzly bear and left to die by his companions.
   1. Wilderness survival — Juvenile literature.
2. Grizzly bear — Legends and stories — Juvenile literature. 3. Glass, Hugh, ca. 1780-ca. 1833 — Juvenile literature. 4. Pioneers — The West — Biography — Juvenile literature. [1. Wilderness survival. 2. Survival.
3. Grizzly bear. 4. Bears. 5. Frontier and pioneer life] I. Shaw, Charles, 1941-   II. Title.
GV200.5.T74   613.6'9   79-21519
ISBN 0-8172-1556-5 lib. bdg.

CONTENTS

Chapter 1   Not So Long Ago 7
Chapter 2   Back to the Wilderness 15
Chapter 3   Left Alone to Die 22
Chapter 4   Surviving the Wilderness 30
Chapter 5   End of a Journey 37
Chapter 6   Meeting with the Deserters 42

Chapter 1
Not So Long Ago

It was not so long ago that the United States was a vast, mysterious forest. Here and there were a few small settlements and a smaller number of cities. The settlers of the 1800s who decided to carve new lives for themselves out of the unfriendly land were a very special breed. Strong and tough, they were willing to face the hard fact that their search for a place to live could lead them to death.

Among the mountain people of the early 1800s, there was one man whose courage and strength were a legend even among the toughest and most skillful woodspeople of the time. That man was Hugh Glass. The story of his incredible journey to safety—a hundred miles alone in the wilderness, badly wounded by a giant grizzly—was told over frontier campfires year after year.

Hugh Glass, the child of Irish immigrants, was a survivor. He was born in the United States in the late 1700s. In his early years he went to sea, and he served as a sailor on a cargo ship in 1820.

Adventure soon singled him out. One night the ship was boarded by a crew of murderous pirates led by the notorious Jean Lafitte.

Lafitte gave the captured crew a choice. They could join his band of smugglers and privateers. Or they would die. Glass and his shipmates chose to join the pirates.

But Lafitte soon saw that his new sailors were just waiting for a chance to take their ship back from the pirates, or somehow get away. He knew that he couldn't trust them in a fight.

One night, Glass and some of his friends were talking quietly among themselves below deck. There, they overheard one of the pirates say that Lafitte had decided to kill them. Now there was only escape—or death! As long as Lafitte thought they were ignorant of their fate, they wouldn't be under watch. In whispers, they plotted their getaway.

Glass's ship was moored for the night off the coast of Texas. Carefully, her captive sailors crept up onto the deserted decks. One by one, they slipped over the side of the ship. All the men were strong swimmers, and the sea was quiet. The coast was near. They could hear the breakers washing on the beach. As Lafitte's men slept on, the kidnapped crew swam toward the shore.

Each man had been able to carry only a few things with him on the swim. They were without food or possessions. At the edge of the beach was an endless forest with its own lurking dangers. After pulling themselves ashore, the exhausted sailors began to walk across country.

A few miles inland the men found a clearing. There they agreed to stop for the rest of the night.

The men awoke as dawn was breaking. Startled, they looked up to find themselves surrounded by Native Americans. They had been stumbled upon by Pawnee scouts. Still weak from swimming and lack of sleep, Glass and his mates were taken to the Pawnee village. There, the tribal elders spoke together. After some talk, it was decided to burn the intruders at the stake.

One by one, the men were marched off and tied to stakes of wood. Brush was piled high around them. The dry tinder was set on fire, and it leaped at their feet. Hugh Glass shuddered at the sound of his friends' screams. His turn was next. Desperate, he cast around for a way to save himself from the horrible fate.

Sticking his hand in his pocket, he pulled out a lump of vermilion. It was a combination of sulfur and mercury used on the ship to color paint. Hugh stared at the brilliant red stuff. Then, on impulse, he offered it to the Pawnee chief. The chief was fascinated by the bright red pigment. Abruptly, he ordered his men to release Glass while he thought about what to do.

Finally, he said he had decided that Glass would be spared because of his handsome gift. As Hugh came to understand that he would live, he became weak-kneed with relief.

He watched as the tribal elders continued to talk. In vain he tried to read the meaning of their words in their gestures and expressions. The group approached. Using hand signs, they explained to Hugh what they had decided. Glass was astonished when he realized that they were

offering to take him into their tribe. They wanted him to join them!

Hugh thought about his alternatives. They all looked pretty dismal. Striking out alone across the wilderness, with no woodland skills, was a death sentence. And death, when it found you, could be slow and painful. "Looks like I'm going to be a Pawnee," he shrugged.

Expressing his thanks for the honor as well as

he could, Hugh Glass joined the Pawnee tribe.

At first, his new life was as strange to Hugh as life on another planet. The woods seemed like a maze. A person could starve to death or be torn limb from limb by the claws of a bear or mountain lion.

For two years, the Pawnee taught Glass how to survive in the wilderness. Though he didn't know it at the time, these lessons would save him more than once in the times ahead. Gradually teaching Hugh their language, the Pawnees took him with them into the forest. They showed him how to read the message of an animal's paw print in the soft ground. By the size, shape, and depth of a print, a Pawnee hunter could tell what kind of animal had made the track, how large it was, how long ago it had passed. These and other signs could lead a sharp-eyed scout to an animal's lair, where there were hides and meat for the people at home.

They knew also which plants were edible. And they knew which were deadly. They knew which of the bright berries were safe to eat. The trees and herbs gave them strong medicines for snakebite and fever.

After two years of life as a Pawnee, Hugh Glass had become at home in the wilderness. But he longed for the more familiar ways of his own people. A prisoner of the forest, he saw little chance of escape.

One day, Hugh learned from a member of the tribe that the chief was planning a visit to St. Louis, Missouri. Hugh went with the group and there seized his chance to get away, disappearing into the crowds of the bustling young city. At last, he was free.

Chapter 2
Back to the Wilderness

Freedom, Hugh soon learned, was hard to get used to. The city seemed like close quarters after living under the sky for two years. And to Hugh it seemed that day to day life in civilization was dull after what he'd been through. He didn't want to go back to sailoring. He thought about the skills he'd learned from the Pawnee. The country needed good trappers and scouts to lead explorers westward.

"Why throw away two years of learning?" Hugh asked himself. Barely a year later, when Hugh picked up the Missouri *Republican* of January 16, 1823, a bold headline on the front page caught his eye. It was an advertisement calling for "100 men to ascend the Missouri River to the Rocky Mountains." Eagerly, Hugh read on. The expedition was to be led by General William Ashley. Able scouts and hunters were needed to lead the way upriver. They planned to leave

March 2 and to journey to a band of trappers who were wintering at Fort Henry at the mouth of the Yellowstone River, under Major Andrew Henry. It didn't take Hugh long to make up his mind. He would go with them! The hundred men with pack horses and equipment set out that spring.

It should have been a tough but predictable trip. However, the other group of trappers up-river at Fort Henry, were having a bad winter. Animals were lost and men had died. General Ashley was surprised when a ragged courier arrived with an urgent plea from Fort Henry.

"We'll never last. That's what the major says.

We need some of your men as replacements, to help us hold the fort. And horses, sir, we need horses just as bad," the courier said.

The group led by General Ashley was now in Arikara territory. The Arikara Indians often traded with the settlers. Ashley knew that the Arikara were sometimes friendly, sometimes hostile. But if conditions at Fort Henry were as bad as the man claimed, Ashley knew he would have to trade with the Arikara for the horses needed at the fort. So he and several men rode to their riverbank village.

The needs of the trappers were explained to the Arikara, and the elders said they had horses they would be willing to trade. But somehow the bargaining went wrong, and the Indians parted with Ashley on unfriendly terms.

Late that night, as dawn was creeping over the sky, the trappers were attacked by Arikara braves.

Hugh Glass was one of the first to awaken to the sounds of war around his bedroll. He grabbed for his rifle and powderhorn. All around him, guns blasted. Angry cries rang out as the awakened trappers returned the attack. The Arikara cut loose many of the trappers' horses and drove them back to their own village.

During the fight, Hugh caught the point of an Arikara knife in his shoulder.

After it was all over, General Ashley walked

among the wounded and dead, taking stock of their situation. Eleven of his men were killed. Thirteen were wounded. They would be unable to resist another attack, should one come.

General Ashley was determined to get back at the Arikara for the deaths of his comrades. He sent one of his few able-bodied men to Fort Henry and demanded help from the major there. "This won't go unpunished," Ashley swore.

Fort Henry recieved the plea, and answered. Along with an officer, Colonel Henry Levenworth, some badly needed men and supplies were sent. The group met with Ashley and planned a counterattack on the Arikara.

The attack was made, and a battle was fought on the banks of the Missouri River. But the Indians were well prepared for war. The trappers fought hard, but not as hard as the Arikara. In the end, it was a defeat for the trappers. Ashley now found himself worse off than before. Out of the 100 men he started with, he had only 30 who were willing and able to continue on to the mountains.

"We'll split into two groups," Ashley ordered. "Some of you will take the supplies upriver by boat to Fort Henry. The rest will go overland and head for the beaver-hunting ground in the Rockies." The land party of thirteen men left with a few packhorses on August 15, 1823. Hugh Glass

was one of the thirteen. For him, it would prove to be an unlucky number, indeed.

The group made its way through the wilderness for about a week, hunting for food along the way. Glass liked to work a little ahead of the rest, by himself. One day he was following a track through the woods when he came to a thicket of bushes along a little stream. He shouldered his way through the thick brush, and came at last into a clearing. There Hugh stopped dead, his heart pounding.

Before him towered a six foot grizzly bear, a mother whose two cubs stared curiously at Hugh. One of the most feared animals in the forest, the

grizzly can break a man's neck with one swipe of a mighty paw. And the fiercest of all grizzlies were the mothers, who would die to protect their cubs. Glass realized he was trapped. He raised his rifle and fired a single shot. With a thundering roar, the bear attacked.

Left Alone to Die

The bear took Hugh's shoulders into her jaws of steel, and he could hear her teeth scraping on his bone. He screamed for help as the bear bit his head and arms. Growling and snapping, the enraged animal shook him like a rag doll. Then her two cubs joined her, and Hugh was suddenly under attack by all three. His rifle lay useless on the bank of the stream where the bear had knocked it. Again and again he screamed as the bear's teeth tore at him.

Some distance behind, his friends heard his cries for help. They followed Hugh's trail through the thicket and into the clearing. Stunned, they saw the bear rising above the helpless man. They raised their rifles and fired. One bullet went through her head, and the bear fell dead upon Glass. It took three of the trappers to drag her huge body from on top of him.

Hugh's rescuers were sure he was dead. But a

faint moan escaped his lips, and they hurried to get him back to camp.

There, General Ashley ordered the men to make a bed for Hugh under the sheltering trees, and to dress his wounds as best they could. Gently, he was washed, and his injuries were bandaged up. Glass himself was unconscious, beyond pain. His fellow trappers spoke in low tones. "I guess old Hugh's seen his last day," said one man.

But at dawn the next day, Hugh was still alive. And that presented a problem. His friends called a meeting to talk it over. Hurt as badly as he was, Hugh couldn't be moved. There was no doctor within two hundred miles. Even if he could survive being carried in a litter, he would slow down the group so much that they'd miss the season for hunting beaver in the mountains. The entire trip would be a failure. There was no other way. Hugh had to be left behind.

But even so, nobody wanted to leave him alone and helpless. General Ashley asked for volunteers to stay with him. Nobody stepped forward. The men were not hard-hearted, but they had to face facts. Anyone who stayed with Glass was in great danger. They would be surrounded by the hostile wilderness. And there was a good chance they would miss the trapping season in the mountains. Then they would lose their entire investment in supplies and time. For a trapper, missing a hunting season meant no money, and a hard winter.

The men decided to take up a collection. They hoped to pay two of their band to stay behind with the dying man and see him decently buried. Every man went through his pockets. At last they pooled eighty dollars, a large sum at that time. An old trapper named John Fitzgerald stepped forward and offered to stay behind. Jim Bridger, a young man who hadn't been trapping for long, also agreed to stay.

The rest of the men broke camp and packed up, grateful they could move on and leave Hugh in good hands. Fitzgerald and Bridger watched them thread their way through the trees. Then they settled in to wait for death to come for Hugh Glass.

Bridger took the first night's watch. He did what he could to make Hugh rest easy, washing his face with cold water from the creek. When Fitzgerald awoke the next morning, Hugh was still alive. He seemed, however, no stronger than before. Bridger stayed in camp while Fitzgerald went out to get some game. He brought back a bird, which they boiled into soup. At night, the two trappers took turns, one sitting up while the other slept. They lived off game they could find close to camp, along with some provisions they had kept.

Incredibly, days passed and Hugh was still alive. Jim Bridger fed him some thin broth with a spoon, and together with Fitzgerald, bathed him. It was the afternoon of the fifth day and Glass was still unconscious. Suddenly, Bridger was startled to see Fitzgerald run into the clearing, his gun in his hand.

"Jim, there have been Arikara nearby. I saw the signs, plain as day."

Jim looked fearfully around. "What'll we do, Fitz?"

Fitzgerald looked over to where Hugh Glass lay. "Well, he's not going anywhere, is he, Jim?"

"No, he's not," the younger man agreed. "But he isn't dead yet, either."

Fitzgerald spat into the fire. "The others didn't mean for us to sit here this long, Jim. I think we have done our duty by old Hugh."

"We can't just leave him here," Jim protested, his eyes wide. "That'd be like murder."

"It'll be murder for sure if those Arikara find us here. And there's nothing we can do for Hugh. Just look at him. He's not long for this world."

Bridger thought it out, frowning. "He came to for a minute today, Fitz. It was while I was trying to feed him."

"He won't come to again. We've got to save our own skins, now. Why, Hugh would be the first one to say so."

Slowly, Fitzgerald won Jim over. They would have to move on and leave Hugh behind. Jim balked, though, when he saw Fitzgerald packing up Hugh's rifle and ammunition.

"We can't leave him here without his gun, Fitz. What if that bear comes back for him?"

"Now, look here, Jim. If we get to the fort without his gun, they're going to ask us why we left a gun with a corpse. And we don't want to have to tell them he wasn't quite dead yet."

"No," Jim agreed.

"Besides," Fitz added, "it goes against the grain with me to throw a good rifle away on a dead man out of principle." He bent over and quickly stripped Hugh of his long, sharp hunting knife. "Might as well take this, too."

As they walked away from Hugh's helpless body only young Jim Bridger looked back. Fitzgerald had taken all the food and ammunition too. Hugh Glass was left lying on a big buffalo hide.

Bridger and Fitzgerald hiked up the Yellowstone River to the fortress at Big Horn. There, they reported that Hugh Glass was dead and buried. Fitzgerald did most of the talking. Bridger hung back, afraid his guilt would show on his face.

People at the fort who had heard of the bear attack weren't surprised to see the two men return alone. It was what they'd expected.

"It was a brave thing you boys did, to stay with the old man," the commanding officer said. Jim shrunk under his praise, but kept his mouth shut. He was as guilty as Fitzgerald. Anyway, even if the story wasn't exactly true, he was sure that Glass was dead by now.

But Jim was wrong about that. Back at the campsite, Glass lay exactly as they'd left him. The small fire had died to grey coals. His chest was still, his last breath seemed spent. His face was pale and slack.

Then, Hugh Glass moved. A groan escaped

him. Slowly, his head began to clear a little. The fog of pain and shock was lifting. He took a gasping breath. Then he moaned again, when the effort of filling his lungs seemed too much to bear. His eyes fluttered open, and he tried to focus. Amazing as it seems, Hugh Glass was still alive.

CHAPTER 4

Surviving the Wilderness

At first all Glass could feel was pain. It was a dull pain that seemed to be all over him. The dullness disappeared, though, when he tried to move, even a little bit. Then, knife-sharp agony stabbed his shoulders and neck as his head moved. Wincing, Glass looked around the empty camp. He frowned, trying to remember. Where was he? Then the memory of the bear attack flooded back to him. He again felt the cold fear in his stomach at the thought of her slashing claws and sharp teeth. His head pounded with pain. With an effort, he licked his dry lips. Where was everyone?

Glass lay for hours, unable to do anything more than look around. The day dragged into afternoon. The slanting shadows gave way to twilight before he began to understand what had happened.

"My God, they've gone and left me," he

thought in horror. Hugh could see that the food was gone. Then, as he slowly turned his head to look around the blanket, sudden terror gripped him. His rifle was gone. Even his powder horn and the little leather pouch for his bullets had been taken.

Rage boiled up inside of him. "The dirty, thieving cowards!" he thought. Somehow he had to face his situation. Grimly, Hugh pushed the cobwebs of pain from his mind. He tried to think clearly. What could he do?

"The worst of it," he thought, "is that they'll get away with it." He could dimly remember that it had been Jim Bridger and Fitzgerald who had stayed with him. The thought of them, safe and well fed, taunted him. It seemed as if he was going to die here for sure, thanks to that bear and the two who had left him here unarmed.

"I'll live to see those two die for what they did, no matter what it takes," Glass swore to himself.

Slowly, he tried to move. Everything hurt at once, and he fell, gasping, back onto the buffalo hide. But he had to try again, and keep on trying. He knew that a little stream ran nearby. He had to have water.

Again, Hugh pulled himself slowly up. He lifted his head to scan the area. Walking, he realized, was out of the question. He could never get to his feet, much less stand. He would have to

crawl. Despite the deep wounds on his shoulders and neck, Hugh began to pull himself along by his arms, dragging his helpless legs. Inch by inch, he fought his way over the few yards to the stream, where the fresh, cool water splashed over the rocks. It seemed like miles to him. His head swam and he became dizzy every few feet. Then, he had to stop and rest until his head cleared. Finally, he made it.

He cupped the water's coolness in his hand, bringing it to his mouth. The sweet water washed down his burning throat, and he sighed thankfully. Strength grew in him, and he looked around at the bushes.

There, growing right by the stream, were berry bushes. And they were covered with ripe, purple blackberries, as long as a man's thumb. When he had drunk enough, Hugh pulled himself over to the bushes. Painfully, he reached for the lowest fruit, and crammed the berries into his mouth. When he'd had his fill, he rested a moment. Then, he pulled himself back over to the stream again. Splashing handfuls of water, he washed the dust and blood from his face. Then he lay back and shut his eyes, exhausted by the effort. Almost immediately he fell asleep, a deep sleep and a long one.

Glass awoke feeling a little stronger. Carefully, he washed the cracked blood off of his arms.

Then he pulled himself back to the berry bushes and ate his breakfast. Afterwards, he started to think.

If he tried to push on to Big Horn, he'd never make it. It was too far. The closest help was back the way he'd come, at Fort Kiowa. But that was over a hundred miles away.

Glass tried to move his legs. But the pain he felt made him light-headed. He knew that walking was impossible. He reached automatically for his knife, and wasn't surprised to find that it was gone, too. "They plucked me clean, those buzzards," he thought. Anger rose to block his pain. For a moment, Hugh sank into despair. He had no weapon to defend himself with. He

was unable to walk. His position seemed hopeless. "I sure wouldn't bet on a broken down old horse like me," he admitted with the ghost of a smile.

Then he began to take stock of his surroundings. There was enough fresh fruit growing within reach to feed him for several days. There was an endless supply of fresh water. Already he felt more alert. Overcoming his despair, Hugh decided to remain by the stream another day or two. He would build up as much strength as he could. The task he had to face seemed beyond him. But he knew it was the only thing he could do. He refused to die. He would crawl the hundred miles and more to Fort Kiowa.

As soon as he felt strong enough, Hugh set out. He traveled at a snail's pace, every inch an act of iron will. Sometimes he passed out from the pain. But when he came to, he doggedly started to inch along again. He pulled himself away from the Missouri River and headed for the Moreau River, miles away across the bluffs and prairies.

The only thing that could possibly save him, the only thing between Hugh Glass and death, was the knowledge of the wilderness he had learned from the Pawnee. And that knowledge did not fail him now.

At night Hugh would crawl into the little spaces under bushes, as a deer would, to sleep.

As he moved slowly along, he stopped now and then to pick wild fruit from a scraggy bush. Sometimes he would wrestle with a leafy weed, pulling it from the soil by its roots. Shaking the dirt from the plant, Hugh would chew on the milky root. He had learned from the Pawnee that the weed was good to eat. As he crawled over the prairie, he kept his eye peeled for one particular weed. It had thick, furry leaves. Finally he spotted one. Quickly, he stripped the dark green leaves from the plant and crammed them into his mouth, ignoring their bitter taste. After a moment he felt a gentle numbness stealing over him. Then he felt a surge of new energy. The medicinal plant was a favorite of the Native Americans, who had discovered its healing powers centuries before. Refreshed, he crawled on, the throbbing pain deadened a little.

CHAPTER 5

End of a Journey

Hugh was still crawling, several days later, when he pulled himself to the top of a little rise to rest and scan the prairie. The land stretched on forever, rolling and grassy. The tall weeds rippled like the ocean in the wind.

His sharp eyes spotted something unusual in the distance. He squinted against the sun to see what it was. A pack of wild wolves were growling and snapping over a dead animal. The wolves, he knew, hunted as a group. But when the hunt was over and the prey brought down, they fought among themselves for the food. When the wolves had finished and moved on, the buzzards would move in and pick over their leavings. Finally the ants would crawl over it, polishing the bones until they gleamed white in the sun. In the wilderness, nature wasted nothing.

Hugh's mouth watered at the thought of meat. "I'll just bust up their little party," he decided. Slowly, quietly, he crawled toward them. As he

went, he picked up stones and pieces of dirt. Suddenly he let out a Pawnee war whoop and hurled the rocks at the startled wolves. They ran off, yelping, as the stones rained around them. Grinning in triumph, Hugh pulled himself toward what was left of their food, a buffalo calf. Normally he didn't care much for raw meat. But this was no time to be picky. With a mumbled prayer of thanks, he ate ravenously. At night he slept beside the calf, guarding his prize. For several days he stayed there, eating what he could and gaining strength. Finally, one day, when he thought he was able, Hugh carefully pulled himself to his feet. Triumphantly he stood, wavering, for the first time since the bear had brought him down. Hugh took his first halting steps. From now on, the going would be easier.

Now that he was upright, Hugh was better able to take food from the forest. But his wounds slowed him down and weren't healing well. He shuffled along the dusty miles, his head drooping. One afternoon a sudden noise ahead of him made him look up sharply. Outlined against the setting sun was a Sioux warrior, staring right at him!

Luckily, Hugh spoke a little of the Sioux language and was able to ask for help. The Sioux were Plains people who hunted buffalo. The brave took the tattered, limping man back to his village. There, Hugh was bathed, and his wounds were dressed. After a few days, he felt much better and was ready to move on. The Sioux gave him food for his journey, and watched as he disappeared over the horizon.

Although he could still make only a few miles a day, Hugh felt refreshed and inspired with new hope. "I'll make it now, for sure," he decided. "And won't those thieving rascals who left me for dead be surprised to see this old ghost!"

Now that he could walk, Hugh was able to put more of his Pawnee knowledge to work. Using the simplest things in the forest—a ropey vine, a slender sapling—Hugh could set a trap that would snare a rabbit as it hopped by. And the fruit he had been feeding on was plentiful this time of year. Hugh gained strength steadily as he walked along. At night he built a campfire to cook whatever small game he'd caught during the day.

Now, too, he was able to scrape together a bed

of leaves at night. Hugh had never gotten used to city comforts. His forest bed suited him. He breathed in the sharp smells of moss and damp earth as he fell asleep. In the morning he awoke to the first glint of dawn and a chorus of birdsong, his body wet with dew. Brushing off the leaves, he stood and stretched, still stiff from his slowly mending injuries. As he moved on, the landscape slowly became more familiar. He knew he was nearing Fort Kiowa.

Finally—after an incredible journey of over 100 wilderness miles—Hugh came to the gates of Fort Kiowa. He called out for help. The gate swung open, and Hugh Glass, his journey ended, stumbled in.

CHAPTER 6

Meeting with the Deserters

When the traders and trappers at Fort Kiowa saw Hugh Glass, they were astonished. He looked as if he'd come back from the grave. And when he told them his story over the first good meal he'd had in over a month, they were even more amazed. Few men would have lived through the attack of the grizzly. But it seemed impossible that Hugh had not only lived, but walked and crawled over 100 miles of dangerous wilderness to safety.

Hugh rested up at Fort Kiowa. Sleeping under a roof and eating regular meals went a long way towards bringing back his shattered health. The trappers urged him to stay on for a while, until he'd gotten back all of his strength. But Hugh was already restless. Somewhere, the two men who had left him to die alone in the wild were living peacefully. Hugh found out they were almost certainly upriver at Major Henry's fort at the Big Horn.

Hugh put together some supplies, including a new rifle and ammunition. He exchanged his tattered clothes for a new set of buckskins. When he heard that a boatload of trappers was stopping at Fort Kiowa the next day, he decided to join them in their trip upriver. "If I wait much longer," he explained, "there's no telling where the rats will get to. I guess I'd better shove off."

The boat made its way upstream as far as a sharp bend in the river, a little below the villages of the Mandan Indians. Glass got out of the boat there to lighten it. He then decided to walk to the fort.

That night he started towards Fort Henry, up the Missouri River to the Yellowstone. The trip took thirty-eight days. Armed and well-prepared for the journey, Hugh found it a far different trip than his first one had been.

When Glass reached Fort Henry, the men there who had been with him in the original group of trappers thought for sure they were seeing a ghost. It didn't take long for Hugh to tell them what had happened after they'd left. In a few minutes, young Jim Bridger, pale as a sheet, was dragged before Hugh Glass, trembling.

But now, in his moment of triumph, Glass

couldn't bring himself to hurt the young man. Bridger pleaded for mercy.

"It was Fitzgerald who made me do it, Hugh! He said he'd leave me there! I never wanted to do it," he sobbed. The picture of revenge that had sustained Hugh Glass across the 100 miles of wilderness faded in his mind. This was no hard-hearted villain. It was just a shivering boy.

Fitzgerald, he understood, was the one who had put the idea into Jim's head. Hugh took up the pursuit of Fitzgerald. He learned the old trapper had gone downriver to Fort Atkinson.

When he arrived at Fort Atkinson, Hugh had every intention of killing Fitzgerald. After all, Fitzgerald's greed had nearly cost Hugh his life. But he did not get the revenge he wanted.

Fitzgerald was now a soldier in the U.S. Army. Killing a soldier was a hanging offense. Hugh thought over the situation. Finally he decided, "I guess the pleasure of putting an end to Fitzgerald isn't worth dangling at the end of a hangman's rope."

He presented himself to Fitzgerald's commanding officer at the fort. The officer listened to his story and called in Fitzgerald. Fitzgerald fell back at the sight of Glass. He would have run if two guards hadn't held him there. Hugh gave him a furious tongue-lashing. "It's only respect for my own life that keeps me from doing to you what you tried to do to me," he finished.

Fitzgerald's officer ordered him to pay for what he had taken from Glass. Hugh, satisfied, moved on the next day.

Hugh Glass's name was a legend in his own day. Because of this he was able to help his fellow trappers when they needed someone to speak up for them. In 1826 the trappers, who risked their lives to bring in furs, rose up against the unfair practices of the fur companies they sold to. Hugh Glass used his reputation and the respect he had won to give their complaints a voice.

But, as always, the forest was his first love. After his brief spell in the public eye, he returned

there. Hugh took a job hunting the big horn sheep at the mouth of the Yellowstone River. It was on a trapping expedition near Fort Cass along the Yellowstone River where Hugh had his final, fatal meeting with the Arikara. He had been hunting beaver and was crossing the iced-over river when he was ambushed and killed.

His name, and the story of his courage, outlived him. As one of his friends remarked, "Hugh had his failings, but his fellow trappers bear testimony to his honor, integrity and fidelity. He could be relied on." In wilderness America—in America of any time—it is hard to think of better words for a man with the courage and endurance of Hugh Glass.